READING ABOUT SCIENCE
Skills and Concepts

John F. Mongillo
Ray Broekel
Beth S. Atwood
Donald L. Buchholz
Albert B. Carr
Claudia Cornett
Jacqueline L. Harris
Vivian Zwaik

Special Reading Consultant
Roger Farr
    Professor of Education
    Indiana University

Phoenix Learning Resources
New York

C

PHOTO CREDITS

ISBN 0–7915–1203–7

(Previously ISBN 0–07–002423–5)

AUTHORS

John F. Mongillo
Editor in Chief, Science Department
Webster Division
McGraw-Hill Book Company
New York, New York

Dr. Ray Broekel
Author and Consultant
Ipswich, Massachusetts

Beth S. Atwood
Writer and Reading Consultant
Durham, Connecticut

Donald L. Buchholz
Developer of Curriculum Materials
Honolulu, Hawaii

Albert B. Carr
Professor of Science Education
University of Hawaii
Honolulu, Hawaii

Claudia Cornett
Assistant Professor of Education
Wittenberg University
Springfield, Ohio

Jacqueline L. Harris
Writer and Science Editor
Wethersfield, Connecticut

Vivian Zwaik
Writer and Educational Consultant
Glen Head, New York

Contributing Writers

Rita Harkins Dickinson
Special Education Instructor
Rio Salado Community College
Phoenix, Arizona

Myra J. Goldberg
Reading Consultant
Rye, New York

Adrienne Ballard Taylor
Junior High School Science Teacher
Black Mountain School
Cave Creek, Arizona

Bruce Tone
Editorial Associate
School of Education
Indiana University
Bloomington, Indiana

Dr. Clifford Watson
Staff Coordinator
Region 1
Detroit Public Schools
Detroit, Michigan

Reviewers

Del Alberti
Principal, John Muir School
Merced, California

Josephine D. Duckett
Elementary Science Resource Teacher
Charlotte-Mecklenburg School System
Charlotte, North Carolina

Dr. Alice Kimber Hankla
Physics Consultant
Atlanta, Georgia

Lola Hanson Harris
Curriculum Specialist
Figueroa Street Elementary School
Los Angeles, California

Jerry Hayes
Science Coordinator
Bureau of Science
Chicago, Illinois

Kent A. Hinshaw
Supervisor of Science
St. Paul Public Schools
St. Paul, Minnesota

Lois Kaylor
Reading Resource Teacher
New Castle Junior High School
New Castle, Delaware

Penny Miller
Reading Specialist
C.E.S.A. 6
Chippewa Falls, Wisconsin

Mary Nalbandian
Director of Science
Chicago Board of Education
Chicago, Illinois

Dr. Martha Piper
Associate Professor of Education
College of Education
University of Houston
Houston, Texas

Dr. Ronald D. Simpson
Professor of Science Education
North Carolina State University
Raleigh, North Carolina

Arlene B. Soifer
Administrator for Educational Programs
Nassau B.O.C.E.S.
Westbury, New York

Patricia Towle
Title I Reading Teacher
McCarthy Elementary School
Framingham, Massachusetts

PRONUNCIATION GUIDE

Some words in this book may be unfamiliar to you and difficult for you to pronounce. These words are printed in italics. Then, they are spelled according to the way they are said, or pronounced. This phonetic spelling appears in parentheses next to the words. The pronunciation guide below will help you say the words.

ă	pat	î	dear, deer, fierce,	p	pop	zh	garage, pleasure;
ā	aid, fey, pay		mere	r	roar		vision
â	air, care, wear	j	judge	s	miss, sauce, see	ə	about, silent
ä	father	k	cat, kick, pique	sh	dish, ship		pencil, lemon,
b	bib	l	lid, needle	t	tight		circus
ch	church	m	am, man, mum	th	path, thin	ər	butter
d	deed	n	no, sudden	_th_	bathe, this		
ě	pet, pleasure	ng	thing	ŭ	cut, rough		
ē	be, bee, easy,	ŏ	horrible, pot	û	circle, firm, heard,		
	leisure	ō	go, hoarse, row,		term, turn, urge,		
f	fast, fife, off,		toe		word		STRESS
	phase, rough	ô	alter, caught, for,	v	cave, valve, vine		Primary stress '
g	gag		paw	w	with		bi·ol'o·gy
h	hat	oi	boy, noise, oil	y	yes		[bī ŏl'ejē]
hw	which	ou	cow, out	yōō	abuse, use		Secondary stress'
ĭ	pit	ōō	took	z	rose, size,		bi'o·log'i·cal
ī	by, guy, pie	ōō	boot, fruit		xylophone, zebra		[bī'elŏj'ĭkel]

TABLE OF CONTENTS

The world of science is a world of observing, exploring, predicting, reading, experimenting, testing, and recording. It is a world of trying and failing and trying again until, at last, you succeed. In the world of science, there is always some exciting discovery to be made and something new to explore.

In this book, you will learn about some of these explorations and discoveries. Through these readings about science, you will have a chance to join the crew of the *Alvin* and explore the strange world beneath the sea. You may hop aboard a hot-air balloon and float across the Atlantic Ocean or track cougars through the Rocky Mountains. You will learn that science is an important part of your life—and that reading about science is fun.

Three Areas of Science

READING ABOUT SCIENCE explores three areas of science: life science, earth-space science, and physical science. Each book in this series contains a unit on each of the three areas. Although there are different areas of science, it is important to remember that each area is related to the others in some way and that all areas are important to people.

Life science is the study of living things. Life scientists explore the world of plants, animals, and humans. Their goal is to find out how living things depend upon each other for survival and to observe how they live and interact in their environments, or surroundings.

The general area of life science includes many specialized areas, such as botany, zoology, and ecology. *Botanists* work mainly with plants. *Zoologists* work mostly with animals. *Ecologists* are scientists who study the effects of air pollution, water pollution, and noise pollution on living things.

Earth-space science is the study of our Earth and other bodies in the solar system. Some earth-space scientists are *meteorologists,* who study climate and weather; *geologists,* who study the earth, the way it was formed and its makeup, rocks and fossils, earthquakes, and volcanoes; *oceanographers,* who study currents, waves, and life in the oceans of the world; and *astronomers,* who study the solar system, including the sun and other stars, moons, and planets.

Physical science is the study of matter and energy. *Physicists* are physical scientists who explore topics such as matter, atoms, and nuclear energy. Other physical scientists study sound, magnetism, heat, light, electricity, water, and air. *Chemists* develop the substances used in medicine, clothing, food, and many other things.

All of these areas of science influence our everyday life. For example, our transportation and communications systems depend on the work of physical scientists. Together, physical scientists, earth-space scientists, and life scientists search for ways to solve problems and improve the quality of our everyday life.

In your reading, you may discover that there is one area of science that you like especially. The bibliography in the back of this book is divided into life, earth-space, and physical sciences. The books that are suggested will take you on more adventures in the world of science.

Reading Science Materials

Some students are nervous about taking courses in science. They think that science is too difficult, and so they give up even before they begin.

Think about this. Do you enjoy the world around you? Do you ever wonder why clouds have so many different shapes and what keeps planes up in the air? Did you ever want to explore a cave or find out why volcanoes erupt or why the earth shakes? If you can answer yes to any of those questions and if you are willing to read and think and investigate carefully the world around you, then you can do well in science and enjoy it, too!

Reading science materials is different from reading a magazine or a novel. You must take your time and think about what you are reading. Remember that science materials contain special vocabulary words. You will know some words. Other words may be familiar to you, but you may be unsure of their meanings. And still other words may be totally unfamiliar. It is these unfamiliar words in particular that make science reading seem difficult.

Steps to Follow

The suggestions that follow will help you use this book:

A. Study the photo or drawing that goes with the story. Read the title and the sentences that are printed in blue. These are all clues to what the story is about.

B.   Study the words for the story in the list of Words to Know in the back of this book. You will find it easier to read the story if you understand the meanings of these words. Many times, you will find the meaning of the word right in the story.

When reading the story, look for clues to important words or ideas. Vocabulary words appear in a special print. Sometimes words or phrases are underlined. Pay special attention to these clues.

C.   Read the story carefully. Think about what you are reading. Are any of the ideas in the story things that you have heard or read about before?

D.   As you read, ask yourself questions. For example, "Why did the electricity go off?" "What caused the bears to turn green?" Many times, your questions are answered later in the story. Questioning helps you to understand what the author is saying. Asking questions also gets you ready for what comes next in the story.

E.   Pay special attention to diagrams, charts, and other visual aids. They will often help you to understand the story better.

F.   After you read the story slowly and carefully, you are ready to answer the questions on the Questions page. If the book you have is part of a classroom set, you should write your answers in a special notebook or on paper that you can keep in a folder. Do not write in this book without your teacher's permission.

Put your name, the title of the story, and its page number on a sheet of paper. Read each question carefully. Record the question number and your answer on your answer paper.

The questions in this book check for the following kinds of comprehension, or understanding:

1. *Science vocabulary comprehension.* This kind of question asks you to remember the meaning of a word or term used in the story.

2. *Literal comprehension.* This kind of question asks you to remember certain facts that are given in the story. For example, the story might state that a snake was over 5 meters long. A literal question would ask you: "How long was the snake?"

3. *Interpretive comprehension.* This kind of question asks you to think about the story. To answer the question, you must decide what the author means, not what is said, or stated, in the story. For example, you may be

asked what the *main idea* of the story is or what happened first, or what *caused* something to happen in the story.

4. *Applied comprehension.* This kind of question asks you to use what you have read to (1) solve a new problem, (2) interpret a chart or graph; or (3) put a certain topic under its correct heading, or category.

You should read each question carefully. You may go back to the story to help you find the answer. The questions are meant to help you learn how to read science better.

G. When you complete the Questions page, turn it in to your teacher. Or, with your teacher's permission, check your answers against the answer key in the *Teacher's Guide.* If you made a mistake, find out what you did wrong. Practice answering that kind of question, and you will do better the next time.

H. Turn to the directions that tell you how to keep your Progress Charts. If you are not supposed to write in this book, you may make a copy of each chart to keep in your READING ABOUT SCIENCE folder or notebook. You may be surprised to see how well you can read science.

Special Sections

There are some special sections that follow each of the three science units.

People to Know is about a person or a group of people who have done something special in the field of life science, earth-space science, or physical science. Some examples are Margaret Seddon, astronaut; Jacques Cousteau, undersea explorer; Benjamin Banneker, astronomer; and Mary Jean Currier, wildlife scientist.

Places to Go takes you on visits to aquariums, zoos, space centers, and museums all over the United States and in Canada.

Puzzles to Do includes crossword puzzles, hidden-word games, and mazes on many different topics in science.

Science Adventures gives you a chance to investigate interesting topics such as solar energy, making fossils, and extrasensory perception.

The last unit in the book is a special unit called Careers in Science. This unit gives you an opportunity to investigate hundreds of science-related careers.

You may decide to make science your lifelong hobby or even your career. Whatever you do, the authors of READING ABOUT SCIENCE hope that this book will help you discover the joys of science.

LIFE SCIENCE

A human skull has 22 bones. Of these 22, 8 bones cover and protect the brain. The other 14 are face bones. Only 1 bone in the skull can move; the others are joined tightly together. Do you know which skull bone is movable? Open your mouth—you moved your jawbone, the only movable bone in the skull.

The Clock of Life

This is one clock that does not tick.

A chicken lays an egg. You feel sleepy. And a tree loses its leaves. All of these things, and many more, happen in a certain way, at a certain time each day or each year. They take place because of something called an *internal clock* (ĭn tûr′ nəl klŏk′). The word *internal* means "inside of," and the internal clock is inside a certain part of every plant and animal. For example, there is an internal clock in the head of a chicken.

The internal clock receives a *signal* (sĭg′ nəl), or message, from the world around it. Some of these signals include light, heat, dark, and cold. When the internal clock gets the signal, the body of the plant or animal produces a chemical that causes the living thing to perform different actions. For example, daylight signals

the chicken's internal clock to make the chemical. Then this chemical causes the chicken to lay eggs.

People are learning a lot about internal clocks. Farmers have even learned how to fool a chicken's internal clock so that the chicken lays more eggs!

14

1. A *signal* is a
   - a. chemical.
   - b. message.
   - c. clock.

2. The clock described in the story is called *internal* because it
   - a. is inside the plant or animal.
   - b. never stops running.
   - c. produces a signal.

3. In this story, one signal would be
   - a. cold weather.
   - b. a chemical.
   - c. falling leaves.

4. In the chain of events below, what is missing?

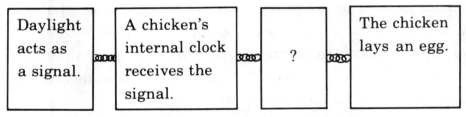

   - a. The chicken is fooled by the farmer.
   - b. The chicken makes a chemical.
   - c. The chicken sees the daylight.

5. What do you think farmers do to make chickens lay more eggs?
   - a. turn on lights in the chicken house at night
   - b. feed the chickens a special chemical
   - c. keep the chickens in a cooler place

Blue whale
107 feet long

Largest Known extinct mammal
(Baluchitherium)

African Elephant

Giraffe

newly born whale calf

Largest Known extinct reptile
(Brachiosaurus)

L·R·B·

Scale drawing showing the Blue Whale as the biggest Mammal there is or ever has been.

The Big One

What is the largest animal ever to live on Earth?

If your answer was the great blue whale, you are right. The blue whale is an air-breathing *mammal* (măm′ əl). A mammal belongs to the group of animals that have fur or hair on their bodies. The females of this group produce milk for their babies. A baby blue whale is almost 7 meters long when it is born, and it drinks about 400 liters of milk a day from its mother. Baby whales are among the fastest-growing animals in the world.

A grown blue whale is about 30 meters long and about 40 times heavier than an elephant. Its body is covered with thick layers of blubber, or fat, and it spends most of its life in the freezing cold waters of the Antarctic Ocean. Blue whales travel in groups called *pods* (pŏdz) and eat *plankton* (plăngk′ tən), tiny plants and animals that float near the surface of the ocean.

The blue whale has been hunted for its meat and blubber, almost to the point of *extinction* (ĭk stĭngk′ shən). Now, people are trying to save this giant of the seas.

1. Tiny plants and animals that float near the surface of the ocean are called

    a. pods.

    b. blubber.

    c. plankton.

2. Which of the following statements is true?

    a. Blue whales travel in groups called pods.

    b. Young blue whales do not grow very fast.

    c. An elephant weighs more than a full-grown blue whale.

3. A baby whale lives *mostly* on _____ during the first year and a half of its life.

    a. its mother's milk

    b. tiny ocean plants

    c. small sea animals

4. What protects the blue whale from the freezing temperatures of the Antarctic Ocean?

    a. its great length of 30 meters

    b. the plankton that it eats

    c. its thick layers of blubber

5. Under which of the following headings would you list the blue whale?

    a. Mammals of the Ocean

    b. Extinct Animals of the Ocean

    c. Cold-Blooded Animals of the Antarctic

The Peregrine Falcon

Why are peregrine falcons in danger of dying out?

Sometimes birds, like the peregrine falcon, eat poisons that are really meant for insects. Once there were peregrines all over the world, but now only a few have survived. What caused the number of peregrines to decline?

The problem began when a *pesticide* (pĕs′ tĭ sīd′) called DDT was sprayed on crops. A pesticide is an insect killer, and the pesticide DDT was used to kill insects that ruined farmers' crops. The poisoned insects were eaten by small birds called quail, and then the peregrine falcons ate the quail.

This continued, and as the DDT filled the body of the falcon, something terrible happened. When the falcons laid their eggs, the shells of the eggs were very thin. So before the baby peregrines were ready to hatch, the shells broke and the baby peregrines died. Now laws against the use of DDT have been passed in the U.S. Scientists have been helping the falcons to find their old homes. In one state alone, Virginia, over 100 falcons have been raised and sent back into the wild. Now there is a good chance that the peregrine falcon will be saved.

1. A *pesticide* is
   a. a baby peregrine falcon.
   b. an insect that eats crops.
   c. an insect killer sprayed on crops.

2. According to the story, farmers used DDT to
   a. protect their crops from insects.
   b. kill birds that were destroying their crops.
   c. destroy the quail.

3. Peregrine falcons are in danger of dying out because
   a. their young die when shells break too early.
   b. they are being sprayed with DDT.
   c. quail are eating the baby peregrines.

4. The shells of the falcons' eggs were thin because
   a. insects were inside the shells.
   b. pesticides were sprayed on the shells.
   c. DDT from the mother's body went into the eggs.

5. Which happened *first*?
   a. The quail ate insects.
   b. The peregrines ate quail.
   c. The farmers sprayed crops.

Sharks!

The great white shark is an ancient and deadly fish.

A *shark* (shärk) is a meat-eating fish that is found all over the world, especially in warm waters. Scientists believe that sharks have lived in the world's oceans for millions of years.

A shark has no bones. Its skeleton is made up of *cartilage* (kär′ tl ĭj), a tough material that stretches like an elastic band.

There are many kinds of sharks. The picture above shows a great white shark. Its body is shaped like a torpedo, and this shape helps the shark swim with great speed.

The white shark is not the largest of all sharks, but it has two rows of sharp, pointed teeth, and it can grow to be more than 12 meters in length. White sharks are known to attack human beings and even small fishing boats.

1. What is *cartilage?*
   - a. the bone in a shark's skeleton
   - b. a tough, elastic material
   - c. a kind of shark

2. Its torpedo shape helps the white shark to
   - a. stretch like an elastic band.
   - b. swim with great speed.
   - c. blow up fishing boats.

3. How are all sharks alike?
   - a. They are white.
   - b. They eat meat.
   - c. They have bony skeletons.

4. Fishers may well fear the white shark's
   - a. huge tail.
   - b. pointed skeleton.
   - c. sharp teeth.

5. Compared with other sharks, the white shark described in the story appears to be
   - a. more dangerous.
   - b. the largest.
   - c. the slowest.

The Flashlight Fish

Have you ever seen a fish with its very own lights?

Some fish have built-in lights. That is, the lights are actually a part of the fish's body! One such fish lives in the Red Sea. It is called the "flashlight fish" because it has special body parts, or *organs* (ôr′ gənz), that give off light.

The flashlight fish has one light organ underneath each eye. These lights are bright and greenish in color, and they are always "on." But a flashlight fish can conceal, or hide, its lights by raising an extra piece of skin up over each organ. Then, when the fish lowers the skin, the lights can be seen again.

What purpose do these special lights have? The light organs help the fish locate food at night along the Red Sea reefs. They also help the fish escape from its enemies. Usually, the lights are flashed "on" and "off" about once every 20 seconds. But when the fish is upset, it will blink its lights about 75 times in 1 minute. Can you imagine 20 or 30 flashlight fish blinking their lights all at the same time?

1. In this story, the word *organ* means
    a. an extra piece of skin.
    b. a special body part.
    c. a kind of eye.

2. The flashlight fish uses its lights to hunt for food and to
    a. change color.
    b. conceal its eyes.
    c. escape from enemies.

3. The flashlight fish gets its name from its
    a. greenish color.
    b. special organs.
    c. unusual eyes.

4. When a flashlight fish is upset, its lights will
    a. be covered.
    b. flash faster.
    c. turn bright green.

5. If a flashlight fish were looking for food at night, it would *probably*
    a. lower its special piece of skin.
    b. turn green in color.
    c. look for flashing lights.

The World's Largest Rodent

What kind of animal looks like a giant rat, swims like a duck, and eats water plants and vegetables?

It is a *capybara* (kăp′ ə bä′ rə), the world's largest rodent. A full-grown capybara can be up to 120 centimeters in length and weigh more than 45 kilograms! This strange-looking rodent has a large, flat head and small, round ears.

Like all rodents, the capybara has strong front teeth that are wide and long and are used to gnaw its food. Its eyes are set so far back on its head that a capybara can't look at anything with both eyes at once.

The capybara's body is fat and covered with hair, and the rodent has almost no tail at all. It has short, strong hind feet and even shorter front feet, which are webbed like a duck's.

Watching capybaras play is great fun, for they love to swim and roll together in warm water. They are friendly animals, but in the United States, you will see them only in a zoo. Most capybaras make their homes in parts of South America, where the water and the weather are often warm.

1. The *capybara* is the world's largest
   a. duck.
   b. rat.
   c. rodent.

2. The body of the capybara is covered with
   a. hair.
   b. fur.
   c. feathers.

3. There aren't many capybaras in the United States because our weather gets too
   a. rainy.
   b. cold.
   c. warm.

4. Which phrase *best* describes the shape of the capybara's body?
   a. long and thin
   b. round and fat
   c. small and flat

5. Why can this strange-looking rodent swim like a duck?
   a. It has a flat head.
   b. Its feet are webbed.
   c. It has almost no tail.

Cry All You Can

Humans are lucky. They can cry.

Tears are a water-like fluid that acts as a built-in eye protector. Without tears, your eyes would be dry and itchy. They wash away dirt and other things that could injure your eyes. Tears contain a special ingredient that destroys germs and protects the eyes against *infection* (ĭn fĕk′ shən).

The scientific name for tears is *aqueous humor* (ā′ kwē əs hyōō′ mər). *Aqueous* comes from the Latin word *aqua,* which means "water." This water-like fluid brings nutrients to the lens and cornea. When the aqueous humor in your eyes overflows,

your eyes begin to water and tear. This happens because there is so much fluid that all of it cannot drain from the tear duct into your nose.

There is aqueous humor behind your eyelid also. There, it slides gently over your eyeball, and each blink of your eyelashes spreads the salty fluid around.

26

1. *Aqueous humor* is the scientific name for _____.

2. The water-like fluid in the eyes contains a special ingredient that
   a. makes the eyes dry and itchy.
   b. protects the eyes from infection.
   c. prevents the fluid from overflowing.

3. Aqueous humor brings _____ to the lens and the cornea.
   a. nutrients
   b. salt
   c. tears

4. What happens when there is too much aqueous humor in your eyes?
   a. The extra fluid drains from the tear duct into your nose.
   b. You can no longer blink your eyelashes.
   c. The extra fluid flows down your cheeks.

5. The *main idea* of this story is:
   a. The water-like fluid in your eyes will remain there for a lifetime.
   b. Aqueous humor will wash, soothe, and guard your eyes.
   c. If you wash your eyes carefully, the aqueous humor will remain forever.

Sea Animal May Help Dentists

From the sea comes a new idea for dentists.

Whirr. Bzzz. Zzzt. At last, the dentist is finished drilling away the *decayed* (dĭ kād′), or bad, part of the tooth. Now there is a large hole, or *cavity* (kăv′ ĭ tē), that has to be filled. The filling the dentist uses should be made of very strong material. It will have to stay in the cavity no matter what kind of food the person eats. The filling will have to remain hard in a place that is always wet. Right now, the fillings dentists use sometimes fall out.

But at the seashore, far from the dentist's office, is an animal that may help solve the problem. This animal is the *mussel* (mŭs′ əl), a tiny sea animal that lives inside two shells. The mussel attaches, or fastens, itself to rocks in the water. It does this with a sticky material that it makes. This sticky material gets very hard and stays strong even in the water. Scientists are performing tests to find out what is in the mussel material and what makes it so strong.

1. According to the story, a *cavity* is a
    a. strong material.
    b. filling.
    c. large hole.

2. A *mussel* is a kind of sea
    a. shell.
    b. rock.
    c. animal.

3. Why does a mussel produce the special material?
    a. to hold its shells together
    b. to fasten itself onto rocks
    c. to fill large holes

4. Why would the material from mussels make a good dental filling?
    a. It would be easy to produce.
    b. It always remains sticky.
    c. It stays hard when wet.

5. Dentists are interested in the mussel material because it is
    a. wet.
    b. sticky.
    c. strong.

Invite a Long Lifetime

Day in and day out, it pumps away. What is it? Your heart.

Your heart is an *organ* (ôr′ gən), a part of your body that performs a very special job. Your heart's job is to pump blood through your body, and it must pump for a lifetime. The way you treat your heart now will affect whether or not it will continue to pump well or develop heart disease. Heart disease includes almost anything that weakens the heart or keeps it from doing its job properly. Both young people and old people are victims of this disease.

What can you do to avoid heart trouble and keep this important organ in top shape? For one thing, you can cut down on the amount of salt that you eat. Salt can cause people to have high blood pressure. Also, don't eat too much butter or too many fatty foods. The excess fat will settle on the walls of the *arteries* (är′ tə rēz) and make it difficult for blood to flow through them. And *do* take time out each day to exercise. The proper amount of exercise makes the heart stronger.

1. A part of your body that does a special job is called an
   _____ .

2. The heart's job is to _____ .

3. According to the story, heart disease can attack
       a. only older persons.
       b. only younger persons.
       c. persons of any age.

4. Doctors would probably advise people with high blood
   pressure to
       a. watch what they eat.
       b. avoid exercise.
       c. do their jobs properly.

Use the table below to answer question 5.

Major Causes of Death in the United States in 1977

Cause of Death	Number of Deaths out of 100,000 People
Cancer	178.4
Heart Disease	331.6
Car Accident	22.3
Pneumonia	22.6

5. The leading cause of death in the United States is
       a. cancer.
       b. pneumonia.
       c. heart disease.

Sauerkraut for Breakfast

History reveals a surprising source of vitamin C.

Vitamins (vī′ tə mĭnz) are substances that are stored in small amounts in plants and animals and are necessary for good health.

One important vitamin that you should have every day is vitamin C. Without it, wounds heal slowly and gums become soft and bleed easily. The body weakens, and it is difficult to fight off sickness. Oranges, grapefruit, and other citrus fruits are vitamin C's best known *sources* (sôrs′ əz). Green peppers and tomatoes also have vitamin C. So do spinach and other green vegetables.

But there is another source of vitamin C that might surprise you. Hundreds of years ago, Viking sea captains kept their crews healthy with *sauerkraut* (sour′ krout′). Sauerkraut is a kind of raw cabbage that is rich in vitamin C and can be eaten hot or cold.

Most people get all the vitamins they need each day by eating a balanced diet. Are you getting the proper amount of vitamins, or do you have a *vitamin deficiency* (vī′ tə mĭn dĭ fĭsh′ ən sē)? To find out, check with your doctor or the school nurse.

1. Substances that are necessary for good health and are stored in small amounts in plants and animals are called _____.

2. What did Viking sailors eat to keep healthy?
   a. plenty of citrus fruits
   b. a kind of raw cabbage
   c. spinach and green peppers

3. According to the story, what are the best known sources of vitamin C?
   a. citrus fruits
   b. vegetables
   c. green peppers

4. The story suggests that vitamin C is good for us because it
   a. protects our bodies from disease.
   b. gives us a lot of energy.
   c. makes us want to eat more.

5. If you have a *vitamin deficiency,* you are probably
   a. eating a balanced diet.
   b. not getting enough vitamins.
   c. taking too many vitamins.

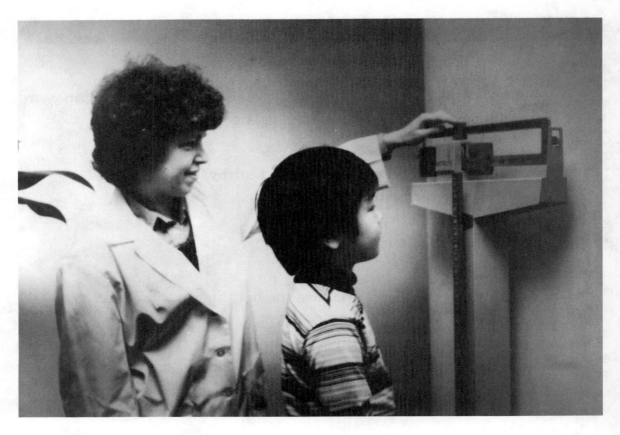

Protecting Your Health

A physical examination is a good way to check up on your health.

It is a good idea to have a *physical* (fĭz' ĭ kəl) examination, or checkup, about once a year. The purpose of the checkup is to make sure that each part of your body is growing and doing its job properly.

During a complete physical examination, your body is checked from head to toe. The doctor uses different kinds of equipment, including a *stethoscope* (stĕth' ə skōp'). This instrument is used to listen to the sounds made by your lungs and heart. A flat wooden stick called a tongue depressor is also used. With it, the doctor can check your tonsils and throat. The doctor checks different parts of your body for lumps or sore spots.

If you are having problems such as not sleeping or losing weight, this is a good opportunity to discuss them with your doctor. It is also a good time to check on the shots you need to protect your body from illness.

1. An instrument used to listen to the sounds made by your lungs and heart is called a _____ .

2. The doctor may use a tongue depressor in order to _____ .

3. You do not have to be sick to have a physical examination.

   a. True

   b. False

   c. The story does not say.

Use the table of abbreviations below to answer questions 4 and 5.

Abbreviation	Meaning	Abbreviation	Meaning
agit. a. us.	shake before using	a.c.	before meals
o.d.	every day	p.c.	after meals
q. 3h	every 3 hours	t.i.d.	3 times a day

4. Which abbreviation tells you to take your medicine before meals?

5. Read the prescription below. Write the meaning of each abbreviation on the line next to the number that matches it.

   Take $\frac{\text{t.i.d.}}{1}$ after meals $\frac{\text{o.d.}}{2}$ for 1 week. Remember to $\frac{\text{agit. a. us.}}{3}$

   1 = _____

   2 = _____

   3 = _____

Chemical Wastes

What can we do about dangerous chemical wastes?

Many of the things we use today were made because of the work of special scientists called *chemists* (kĕm′ ĭsts). A chemist makes and uses special materials called *chemicals* (kĕm′ ĭ kəlz), which are then used to make products such as paints, dyes, paper, and certain types of clothes. Often, there are some chemicals left over after these products are made. These leftover, or unused, chemicals are called *chemical wastes* (kĕm′ ĭ kəl wāsts).

What happens to chemical wastes? For a long time, chemical wastes have been buried in the ground or dumped in rivers, streams, and oceans, and no one has worried about the dumping until now. Now, we know that certain chemical wastes can make people and other living things sick.

People are working to pass laws to stop the dumping of chemical wastes, and some companies are looking for safer ways to dispose of them. Also, scientists are testing ways to use leftover chemicals to make other useful products.

1. *Chemical wastes* are

   a. materials for clothes.

   b. leftover chemicals.

   c. chemicals that have been used up.

2. According to the story, for a long time chemical wastes have been _____ .

3. Today, we know that chemical wastes can

   a. never be used again.

   b. be harmful to all living things.

   c. be dumped safely in rivers or streams.

4. In the story, one way to lessen the dangers from chemical wastes is

   a. to bury chemicals very deep in the ground.

   b. to find a way to make fewer products.

   c. to make the dumping of wastes unlawful.

5. Which one of the following statements is true?

   a. All chemicals are poisonous.

   b. Scientists called chemists have stopped making chemicals.

   c. Chemicals are an important part of our lives.

The Hardiest Weed of All

Gardeners spend hours trying to get rid of it!

In spring, its sunny yellow head can be seen almost everywhere. This little yellow flower is a weed called the *dandelion* (dăn′ dl ī′ ən). Once started, it spreads quickly and is very hard to control.

The dandelion is a *perennial* (pə rĕn′ ē əl), which means that its leaves and flowers die but its roots live on from year to year. Chopped off at the ground, this hardy perennial will grow again in one to two weeks and will often grow two plants in place of one.

The head of the dandelion is really a tight little cluster of 150 to 200 flowers. When the flower cluster dies, it forms a fluffy gray ball, which holds the plant's seeds. There is one seed for every flower in a cluster. A light wind can carry the seeds about 1500 centimeters. Is it any wonder that gardeners think of the dandelion as a pest?

1. A plant whose leaves and flowers die but whose roots live on from year to year is called a

    a. seed.

    b. perennial.

    c. cluster.

2. When chopped off at the ground, the dandelion will

    a. die in one to two weeks.

    b. grow again in one to two weeks.

    c. grow again the following spring.

3. The head of the dandelion is really a

    a. cluster of yellow flowers.

    b. fluffy gray ball.

    c. group of small yellow leaves.

4. What makes the dandelion hard to control?

    a. Its flowers die and come back the next year.

    b. Its leaves can grow in one to two weeks.

    c. Its seeds get scattered easily.

5. Under which of the following headings would you list the dandelion?

    a. Gray Flowering Plants

    b. Seedless Perennials

    c. Perennial Pests

Red Seaweed

An ocean weed is used in making many products.

What do we get from the oceans of the world? All kinds of fish, yes, but we also get a plant called *seaweed* (sē′ wēd′). One type of seaweed is red in color and grows to be about 1 meter in length.

When we think of a weed, we think of a useless, unwanted plant. But seaweed can be used for many purposes. One important product obtained from red seaweed is *agar* (ā′ găr). Scientists use agar in many ways, including the making of certain foods such as candy. Agar is also used in making some medicines.

One kind of red seaweed that is rich in agar is found off the island of Japan. Divers collect this seaweed and load it onto boats. When a boat is full, it returns to shore, where the seaweed is unloaded and spread out to dry in the sun. When completely dry, it is gathered up into bundles and shipped to a factory. At the factory, agar is made from the seaweed.

The next time you buy candy, read the ingredients on the wrapper. You may find agar listed!

1. What is *agar?*
    a. red seaweed
    b. a product made from seaweed
    c. a kind of medicine

2. The red seaweed used to make agar is gathered by
    a. fishers.
    b. scientists.
    c. divers.

3. Besides growing in the ocean, seaweed is different from most weeds because it can
    a. grow tall.
    b. be useful.
    c. turn red.

4. Before we can get agar from it, the seaweed *must* be
    a. dyed red.
    b. completely dried.
    c. sent to Japan.

5. What is the *main idea* of this story?
    a. Using seaweed is too much trouble.
    b. Seaweed can be very valuable.
    c. Japan depends on seaweed.

Tree Rings

You can find out many things about a tree by studying its rings.

Each year, from top to bottom, a tree wraps a new layer of wood around itself. If you cut across a tree trunk or branch, you would see that these layers of wood look like rings. By counting *tree rings* (trē rĭngz), you can tell how old the tree is. If you count ten rings, for example, the tree is ten years old.

Looking at the picture shown above, you can see that each tree ring has a dark section and a light section. The light wood grows in the spring, the dark wood in the summer. Observe, also, that some rings in the picture are wide and others are narrow. Trees grow wide rings during the years when they get a lot of moisture and sunlight. By examining tree rings, you can tell what the weather may have been like many years ago.

Giant sequoia trees, such as the one in the photo above, grow in northwestern California. Some of these sequoias have more than 3,000 tree rings. Can you guess how old such a tree would be?

1. According to the story, a *tree ring* is a
   - a. branch.
   - b. layer of wood.
   - c. giant sequoia.

2. A tree ring is added to a tree
   - a. every ten years.
   - b. every year.
   - c. every 3,000 years.

3. The light part of a tree ring
   - a. gets dark in the winter.
   - b. tells the tree's age.
   - c. grows in the spring.

4. From the story, you can tell that
   - a. all tree rings look the same.
   - b. most trees do not grow tree rings.
   - c. tree rings add to the tree's width.

5. Look at the drawing below. If this were a slice from a tree trunk, how old would the tree be?
   - a. five years old
   - b. five months old
   - c. six years old

Life in the Forest

Animals depend upon one another for food.

There are many kinds of animals that live in the forest, such as mice, rabbits, squirrels, owls, and hawks. Animals in the forest depend upon one another for food.

Many small forest animals, such as mice, eat green plants for food, and then they, themselves, are eaten by larger animals. This is called a food chain.

A food chain begins with the sun. The green plants in the forest use the sun's energy to make food for themselves. This process, or action, is called *photosynthesis* (fō′ tō sĭn′ thĭ sĭs).

Forest plants produce flowers and seeds that are eaten by mice and other animals. The mice get their energy from the plants, and the mice become food for a larger animal, such as the hunting hawk. So the energy from the sun passes from the plants to the mice to the hawk. A break in any link of this food chain means that some animal may not have enough food to survive.

1. *Photosynthesis* takes place when
   - a. green plants use the sun's energy to make food.
   - b. forest animals eat the food made by green plants.
   - c. the food chain is broken.

2. What is the *first* link in a food chain?
   - a. the sun
   - b. green plants
   - c. forest animals

3. Animals sometimes cannot find enough food because
   - a. there is very little food in a forest.
   - b. photosynthesis stops.
   - c. there is a break in the food chain.

4. What does the food chain show about living things?
   - a. that they depend upon each other
   - b. that small animals eat as much as large animals
   - c. that plants with flowers are most important

Which of the living things below fills the missing link in this food chain?

| sun's energy | — | ? | — | squirrels | — | hawks |

   - a. mice
   - b. green plants
   - c. owls

Watch Out for Poisonous Plants

Don't touch! That plant is poisonous!

Did you know that in the United States there are almost 400 kinds of *poisonous* (poi′ zə nəs) plants? A *poison* is any substance, or material, that causes injury, illness, or death. Perhaps you have heard of poison ivy and poison oak. These plants are found in North America. By touching them, a person can get an annoying and sometimes painful skin condition that is called *dermatitis* (dûr′mətĭ′tĭs). Dermatitis causes the skin to get red and itchy and develop watery blisters.

Poison ivy grows in the form of a bush or a vine. It has small green flowers and white berries. The plant's leaves grow in groups of three, and they can be smooth and shiny or hairy.

What should you do about poisonous plants? Find out what kinds of plants grow in your neighborhood. Learn to recognize plants like poison ivy and poison oak, which grow freely in many places.

1. A *poison* is any substance that
   a. causes illness, injury, or death.
   b. is found in plants with groups of three leaves.
   c. grows freely on vines in North America.

2. One way to recognize poison ivy is by its
   a. hairy flowers.
   b. white berries.
   c. four leaves.

3. When people get dermatitis from poison ivy, what might they notice *first*?
   a. smooth, shiny skin
   b. watery blisters
   c. red, itchy skin

4. The *main purpose* of this story is to tell the reader how
   a. to find poisonous plants.
   b. important it is to recognize poisonous plants.
   c. to treat diseases caused by poisonous plants.

5. Under which of the following headings would you list poison ivy?
   a. A Leafless Vine
   b. A North American Plant
   c. A Poisonous Fruit

The Misunderstood Spider

How much do you really know about spiders?

Spiders are misunderstood animals. For one thing, they are not really insects, as most people think. Insects have six legs, while spiders have eight. And spiders have only two body parts, the head and the *abdomen* (ăb' də mən). Insects have a third part, called the *thorax* (thôr' ăks').

Of the 30,000 different kinds, or *species* (spē' shēz'), of spiders, only some spin webs. All spiders produce silk, but each species has its own way of using the silk. The web spinners weave silky webs in order to catch food. The best-known web is the circular, or round, web spun by the garden spider. Other spiders may make nets to drop over their victims. One species even sends out a single sticky strand of silk like a fishing line to catch its food. When a fly gets stuck to the end of the line, the spider hauls in its "fish."

1. Each different kind of spider is a different _____ .

2. According to the story, web spinners use their silky webs to
   a. sleep in.
   b. catch food.
   c. hide themselves.

3. How many body parts do spiders have?
   a. two
   b. three
   c. six

4. The story leads you to believe that some spiders eat
   a. fish.
   b. flies.
   c. people.

5. Another title for "The Misunderstood Spider" might be
   a. "Not Really an Insect."
   b. "A Useless Insect."
   c. "Common Garden Insects."

Dr. Charles Drew
(1904—1950)

Place your hand in the center of your chest. What do you feel? Of course, you feel a thumping. The thumping is the force of the heart pumping blood through your body. Without blood being pumped through your body, you would soon die. For many years, scientists have studied blood and the way it circulates through the body. One important person in the area of blood research is a scientist named Charles Drew.

Charles Drew was a man with many abilities. He was an excellent student and an outstanding athlete during his years at Amherst College in Massachusetts. After graduation, he enrolled in medical school. He then went on to become a brilliant scientist and surgeon.

While attending medical school in Canada, Drew made a discovery that would save many lives. He found out that *plasma* (plăz′ mə) could be used to replace whole blood. Plasma is the clear, yellowish, liquid part of the blood. Drew discovered that plasma could be stored for long periods of time in refrigerators. This meant that a hospital could keep a supply of blood on hand, ready for use. In 1940, Dr. Drew set up and directed the British Blood Bank. Blood collected in New York was sent to England. Because of Charles Drew's work, millions of lives have been saved all over the world.

A Visit to the New England Aquarium

Do you know that some fish change colors in minutes? Penguins can swim underwater very fast? Some kinds of sharks are only 10 centimeters long?

You can see these animals and many more at the New England Aquarium in Boston, Massachusetts. The aquarium was built to give visitors a view of the animals that live in the world of water.

Visitors can see more than 2,000 sea animals at the aquarium. The animals live and swim in a large number of water tanks. The tanks hold fresh-water and saltwater animals. The largest glass wall tank holds sharks, huge green turtles, and schools of striped bass. Penguins, otters, and harbor seals are the most popular animals at the exhibits.

The aquarium has special water shows, too. In one show, visitors can watch sea lions and dolphins doing tricks. The show helps visitors see how strong and how smart the animals are.

Endangered and Threatened Wildlife

Find the names of 17 animals that are listed as endangered or threatened. The names are hidden across and down, and two names are written diagonally. For help, use the list of animal names below.

Word List

GORILLA
BOBCAT
CHEETAH
TIGER
TORTOISE
ALLIGATOR
PEREGRINE FALCON
BLUE WHALE
SPERM WHALE
GRAY BAT
GAZELLE
BALD EAGLE
KIT FOX
COUGAR
LEOPARD
OCELOT
JAGUAR

```
K L E O P A R D B O
I C H E E T A H B S
T I G E R T I G A P
F B L U E W H A L E
O I O J G G G L D R
X G T A R A O L E M
O R T G I Z R I A W
C A O U N E I G G H
E Y R T E L L A L A
L B T J F L L T E L
O A O O A E A O K E
T T I B L G L R I G
O I S E C O U G A R
M G E A O A G A L E
S P E A N B T O R S
```

The Human Body

Fill in the spaces with the names of 14 parts of the human body. The words are given to you below.

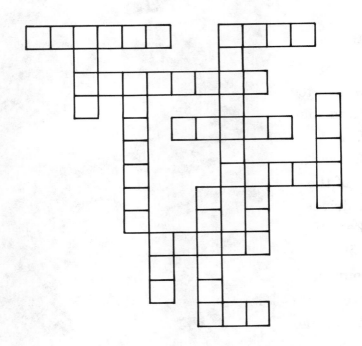

3-Letter Words

lip

ear

4-Letter Words

eyes

nose

skin

5-Letter Words

mouth

heart

brain

lungs

6-Letter Words

finger

tongue

7-Letter Words

stomach

eardrum

8-Letter Word

skeleton

Measuring Reaction Time

Reaction time is the length of time needed to make a decision and then do something. For example, a driver sees a ball roll in front of the moving car. The driver jams on the brakes. If the car is going 50 kilometers per hour, it will move about 10 meters during an average driver's reaction time.

In this science adventure, you are encouraged to investigate reaction time. But since reaction time is often less than a second, it will be very difficult to use a time unit. Instead of a time unit to describe reaction time, you will use a distance unit—the number of centimeters an object falls.

You will need a partner in this adventure. Compare your reaction time with your partner's. With other classmates'.

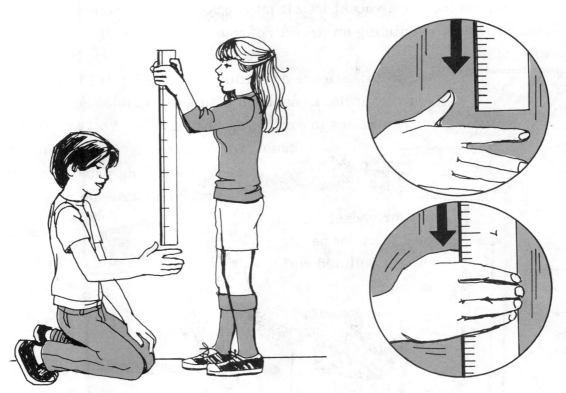

To participate in this science adventure, you will need a meter stick and a partner.

Hold your right hand out with your thumb and forefinger about 3 centimeters apart. Have your partner hold a meter stick in between your fingers. Make sure the stick does not touch you.

Look at the bottom of the meter stick, not at your partner. When you are ready, your partner should drop the stick and you should catch it. The number of centimeters the stick falls before you catch it gives a good indication of your reaction time.

Try the same thing several times. Does your reaction time vary?

Try your left hand. How do your reaction times compare with those for your right hand?

Now let your partner determine his or her reaction times.

Investigating a Vacant Lot

Take a good look at a vacant lot. It may look vacant, or empty, because there is no building on it. But, of course, it isn't really empty, is it?

In this science adventure, you are invited to examine a vacant lot in as much detail as possible. Some questions to explore are listed here. You will no doubt think of others. You do not have to do everything listed here. But once you start, you may find it hard to stop!

Is your vacant lot a good place for people? Or is it polluted with garbage?

What animals are permanent residents in your vacant lot? What animals are just passing through?

What kinds of animal life can you find in the grass? In trees? Under rocks? In a rotting log?

What trees are in your vacant lot?

What birds are in your vacant lot?

How does your vacant lot change in summer, fall, winter, spring?

What kinds of plant life are in your vacant lot? Any poisonous plants? Weeds? Flowers?

What different kinds of seeds can you find in your vacant lot?

EARTH-SPACE SCIENCE

Have you ever heard of an underwater well? There are many such oil wells. Oil forms underground. It may be found under farmland, jungles, swamps, or mountains. Large amounts of oil are found in the earth under the ocean's bottom. This oil well in the Gulf of Mexico has created a gusher. Gushers are rare today, because scientists have found ways to control the flow of oil as it comes out of the well.

Tornado Warning!

There can be danger in a dark spring sky.

People stop what they are doing and quickly go to a shelter, or safe place, when they hear the siren. The siren is a warning that a *tornado* (tôr nā′ dō) is coming.

A tornado is a storm that usually occurs in the spring and early summer months in certain parts of the world. A tornado covers only a small area. But, it can destroy everything in its narrow path, because the winds of a tornado spin very fast.

What causes the winds to move so fast? When cold air sinks and warm, wet air rises, winds begin to spin. As the winds spin faster, more warm air is pulled upward. Then, cold air moves in under the warm air. If this action continues over and over, a large, funnel-shaped cloud soon rises up into the sky. The pointed end of the funnel rushes along the ground, sucking up everything in its way. A tornado can destroy an entire town and kill many people. But people who hear and obey the warning can be saved.

1. A *tornado* can easily be identified by its
   a. slowly rising temperatures.
   b. large, funnel-shaped cloud.
   c. noisy, siren-like winds.

2. According to the story, a tornado usually takes place in the _____ or early summer.

3. According to the story, which of the following statements about a tornado is true?
   a. It always covers a very wide area.
   b. It can destroy everything in its narrow path.
   c. It usually occurs at any time all over the world.

4. Paragraph 3 leads you to believe that
   a. warm air is lighter than cold air.
   b. warm air is pulled downward by spinning winds.
   c. when cold air moves up, warm air comes in.

5. What part of a tornado actually causes the damage?
   a. the cloud
   b. the spinning winds
   c. the warm, wet air

Nature's Deep Freeze

What happened during the Great Ice Age?

Thousands of years ago, the winters began to get colder and the summers grew shorter until there were no summers at all. This was a period known as the Great Ice Age. Snow piled up 15 stories high over much of the Northern Hemisphere. Under the weight of so much snow, an ice pack formed and began to push forward. At that point, a *glacier* (glā′shər) was born.

As it moved slowly down the mountains, the glacier buried unlucky animals that were trapped in cracks in the earth. There they remained, perfectly frozen, for thousands of years.

Then, slowly, the climate changed, and the glacier began to melt. About 100 years ago, scientists made an amazing discovery. They found a wooly mammoth that had been preserved intact in the "deep freeze" for 10,000 years!

1. A mass of thick moving ice is called a _____.

2. What happened during the period in history called the **Great Ice Age?**
   - a. Winters began to get colder.
   - b. The climate began to get warmer.
   - c. A huge mountain of snow began to melt.

3. According to the story, which of the following statements is true?
   - a. Animals buried by the glacier remained frozen for thousands of years.
   - b. It takes very little snow to form an ice pack.
   - c. A glacier moves very quickly as it pushes forward.

4. Because our weather today is warmer than it was thousands of years ago,
   - a. there are many more wooly mammoths.
   - b. there are fewer glaciers.
   - c. it no longer snows in the Northern Hemisphere.

5. The story says that the wooly mammoth had been frozen for 10,000 years. Therefore,
   - a. scientists must have discovered the animal 10,000 years ago.
   - b. the animal must have been 10,000 years old when it was caught in the ice.
   - c. the glacier had to be at least 10,000 years old.

Fossils of Ocean Animals

Why do scientists think the middle of North America was once under a warm sea?

Today, Missouri, Kansas, Nebraska, Iowa, and Indiana are hundreds of miles from an ocean. Yet scientists have found evidence, or proof, that *marine* (mə rēn'), or sea, life once lived in each of these five states. The evidence is in the form of *fossils* (fŏs'əlz), the remains of plants or animals that lived millions of years ago and are often found preserved in certain kinds of rock.

Fossil hunters discovered the remains of marine animals without backbones, including sea snails and clams. Some fossils were perhaps 500,000,000 years old! They also found fossils of marine life with backbones, such as sea turtles, crocodiles, and bony fish.

Some fossil marine animals, such as starfish and clams, are easy to recognize. But others look like beautiful flowers with stems and buds. These sea lilies, or *crinoids* (krī'noidz), still live today in warm sea waters and use their petal-like arms to catch tiny sea animals for food. The state of Iowa is famous for its fossil crinoids.

1. *Marine* life is life that exists _____.

2. Which of the following is proof that the middle part of North America was once underwater?
   - a. marine fossils
   - b. certain kinds of rock
   - c. live crinoids

3. Crinoids are known as sea lilies because they are
   - a. actually underwater flowers.
   - b. so easy to recognize.
   - c. shaped like flowers.

4. The fossil crinoids found in Iowa show that long ago the state was
   - a. probably under a sea of warm water.
   - b. covered with layers of rock.
   - c. only a few hundred miles from the ocean.

5. Under which of the following headings would clams belong?
   - a. Marine Life without Backbones
   - b. Underwater Plant Life
   - c. Fossils with Stems

Jupiter's Moons and How They Travel

The many moons of Jupiter travel around the planet in different directions.

Jupiter is the largest planet in our solar system. Over the years, scientists have found that Jupiter has its own small solar system. Earth has one moon. Jupiter has at least sixteen and probably more.

Since there are so many moons, scientists began to number them. The numerals tell the sequence, or order, in which the moons were found. They were slower to name the moons. All of Jupiter's moons now have a name as well as a number.

The first five moons to be discovered are known as the "inner moons." But they are not the closest to the planet. The closest is only 127,600 kilometers away from Jupiter. All the inner moons circle the planet *counterclockwise* (koun'tər

klŏk'wīz') direction, that is, opposite of the hands of a clock.

Jupiter's middle group of moons are at least 11,100,000 kilometers from the planet. They also move in a counterclockwise motion. The four farthest moons are at least 20,700,000 kilometers away. These are called "outer moons." They circle in a clockwise motion.

How many more moons do you think will be discovered?

1. Things that travel in the same direction as the hands of a clock are said to be traveling in a
   - a. clockwise direction.
   - b. counterclockwise direction.
   - c. different direction.

2. Jupiter's _____ group of moons travel in a clockwise direction.
   - a. inner
   - b. middle
   - c. outer

3. The numbers given to Jupiter's moons tell
   - a. the order in which they were discovered.
   - b. the order in which they travel.
   - c. the order of their distance from Jupiter.

4. According to the story, which of the following statements is true?
   - a. None of Jupiter's moons have names.
   - b. Most of Jupiter's moons circle clockwise.
   - c. Jupiter's inner moons were discovered first.

5. Use the three lines below to show how far away each group of moons is from Jupiter.

   Inner Group: _____ kilometers

   Middle Group: _____ kilometers

   Outer Group: _____ kilometers

The Moon Named Io

Voyager 1 *takes pictures of Jupiter's moons.*

In 1979, the spacecraft *Voyager 1* took thousands of pictures of the planet Jupiter. It also took many pictures of Jupiter's moons. A moon is a *satellite* (săt′l ĭt′), that is, a body that travels in a path around a larger body, or planet.

One of Jupiter's moons, or satellites, is named *Io* (ī ō) and is about the same size as Earth's moon. But, unlike our moon, Io has almost no craters, or large holes, on it.

Scientists once thought that Io would be like Earth's moon—cold and without much color. But photographs sent back by *Voyager 1* show that Io is a bright orange-red color with patches of white here and there. The photos of Io also show that there are many volcanoes on it and that quite a few of these are active. That is, gas and other materials shoot out of the volcanoes.

The volcanoes on Io appear to be more powerful than those found on Earth. So far, Jupiter's moon Io and our planet Earth are the only known bodies in space that have active volcanoes.

1. A body that travels in a path around a larger body, or planet, is called a
   a. volcano.
   b. satellite.
   c. crater.

2. Earth's moon is about the same size as
   a. Jupiter.
   b. Io.
   c. Voyager 1.

3. Scientists once believed that
   a. Earth was one of Jupiter's moons.
   b. Io was cold and had little color.
   c. Earth's moon had active volcanoes on it.

4. Besides being bigger, how is Jupiter *unlike* Earth?
   a. It has more than one moon.
   b. It is red with white patches.
   c. It has active volcanoes.

5. What is it about Earth and Io that makes them different from any other bodies in space?
   a. They both have active volcanoes.
   b. They both have many craters.
   c. They are both bright red in color.

The Planet Mercury

Mercury is one of the hottest planets in our solar system.

Mercury (mûr′kyə rē) is the closest planet to the sun. The surface temperature during Mercury's sunlit day is over 420°C, but at night, the temperature drops to below −170°C. A day on Mercury lasts about 1,416 Earth hours! Mercury is also the fastest planet in our solar system, because it takes Mercury just 88 days to revolve around the sun. It takes planet Earth about 365¼ days to revolve around the sun.

Most of the time, Mercury is difficult to see from Earth because of the sun's brightness. Therefore, not very much was known about Mercury's surface until 1974, when the spacecraft *Mariner 10* began taking pictures of the planet. The pictures show that there are many *craters* (krā′tərz), or large holes, on the planet that may have been made when objects from space hit Mercury's surface. Mercury has mountains, hills, and valleys, and its surface is covered with rocks. *Mariner 10*'s pictures show that Mercury's surface is very much like our moon's surface.

1. According to the story, a *crater* is a
   a. spacecraft.
   b. large hole.
   c. small planet.

2. How long is a day on Mercury?
   a. 88 Earth days long
   b. about 1,400 Earth hours long
   c. equal to 1 day on Earth

3. The surface of Mercury is said to be
   a. very flat.
   b. like the sun's surface.
   c. like Earth's moon.

4. Why is it that humans could not live on Mercury?
   a. It moves too fast.
   b. It gets too hot and too cold.
   c. It has too many craters.

5. Based on the information in the story, what might Mercury be called?
   a. The Darkest Planet
   b. The Hidden Planet
   c. The Slowest Planet

Meteorites: Space Rocks That Fall to Earth

Nickel-Iron [Mete]orite (Siderite)
SANDIA MTS., New Mexico
Found about 1915
Total known weight 14 kg. (31 lb.)
Nininger Collection

What are meteorites? How can you tell them from Earth rocks?

A *meteorite* (mē'tē ə rīt') is rock-like matter that has fallen to Earth from space. Most meteorites look just like Earth rocks, but a meteorite the size of an orange weighs much more than an Earth rock of the same size. Meteorites can be many shapes and sizes. They can be as small as a peanut or as large as a truck.

Most meteorites are dark brown on the outside, and since most of them contain metal, they are silver or gray inside. Meteorites found on Earth are almost all metal inside and are known as iron meteorites. Other meteorites are made of stone or are a mixture of stone and metal. Iron meteorites are found more often because they are the least likely to break apart while falling through space or when hitting Earth.

Most stony Earth rocks do not contain metal. So if you think you have found a meteorite, check it with a magnet. If the magnet sticks to the rock, you may have found a space rock that has fallen to Earth!

1. Rock-like matter that has fallen to Earth from space is called a
   a. magnet.
   b. meteorite.
   c. metal.

2. A meteorite the size of an orange will weigh _____ an Earth rock of the same size.
   a. less than
   b. much more than
   c. about the same as

3. If you found a meteorite, what color would it probably be?
   a. silver
   b. gray
   c. brown

4. A magnet will help you tell a stony Earth rock from a meteorite, because the magnet will
   a. stick to the stony Earth rock.
   b. stick to the meteorite.
   c. show which rock weighs more.

5. The biggest meteorites found are likely to contain more
   a. iron than stone.
   b. silver than iron.
   c. stone than metal.

Fog

Should fog be welcomed or feared?

We usually think of *fog* (fôg), with its cloud-like, moist air, as scary and troublesome. But fog can be good as well as bad. The fine water droplets in a fog layer gently moisten plants and soil.

Winter fog forms as a result of warm raindrops falling through colder air. Winter fog sometimes acts as a blanket that keeps the warm air "tucked" close to the ground. Fog may protect gardens from frost and keep buildings warm. Then less heating fuel is needed. In summer, a fog may block out sunshine, keeping the air at the ground level cool and moist.

Unfortunately, fog can also be dangerous. Heavy fog makes it difficult to see more than a few meters. Also, fog changes the way that sound travels. It causes sound waves to bounce up so high in the air that they skip over large areas without being heard. This problem is very noticeable over large bodies of water. Sometimes foghorns and breaking waves cannot be heard. Danger can be close at hand, but neither sight nor sound gives a warning.

1. *Fog* is the word used to describe a cloud-like layer of air made up of fine _____ droplets.

2. Winter fog is formed when
   a. warm raindrops fall through colder air.
   b. cold air sinks to ground level.
   c. warm air acts as a blanket.

3. A heavy fog makes it difficult to
   a. keep the ground moist.
   b. see more than a few meters.
   c. keep warm air at ground level in winter.

4. Which of the following describes one way in which fog is good?
   a. Fog acts as a watering system for plants and soil.
   b. Fog decreases the noise level over large bodies of water.
   c. Fog develops only during the summer months, when the air is warm.

5. Which one of the following people would probably welcome fog?
   a. a sailor
   b. a gardener
   c. a driver

Digging Up the Past

Do young people really "dig" the past? Some do. They become helpers at archaeological *digs*. There, the teenagers help scientists called archaeologists sift through the ruins of the past. They look for the remains, or what is left, of past human activities. The remains may include old bones, buildings, tools, or pottery.

Some teenagers are chosen each year to help in summer science projects with *Earthwatch*. Earthwatchers look for dinosaur bones in South Dakota. They go to faraway countries to work. And still other teenagers help scientists learn more about how Native Americans lived long ago.

The teenagers work hard. Sometimes they are helping when a real treasure is found—a bone or a complete pottery bowl. But days, even weeks, go by when the scientists and their teenage helpers carefully sift through layers of earth and find nothing.

Other young people who cannot go on special projects such as *Earthwatch* go to digs in their home states. And sometimes whole families go together to help archaeologists dig up the past to find out more about the animals and people who lived in the United States long, long ago.

A Visit to the Reuben H. Fleet Space Theater and Science Center

One of the most modern space theaters in the world is in San Diego, California. It is called the Reuben H. Fleet Space Theater and Science Center. Each year, many people visit the Space Theater to learn about outer space.

The Space Theater has special movie machines. The machines show the movements of the sun, moon, planets, and stars on the surface of a dome. The dome is a huge rounded movie screen. One of the machines, the Star Ball, can show more than 10,000 stars on the surface of the dome!

Special films help make visitors feel like they are really traveling to outer space. In one film, visitors fly through the mysterious clouds of Venus.

The Space Theater has "see-touch-hear" exhibits. In one exhibit, a visitor can listen to her or his own heartbeat. Other exhibits are on light, simple machines, waves, sound, and solar energy.

PUZZLES TO DO

Oceans

Do you like the ocean? This puzzle contains words that are related to the ocean. If you need help, use the words listed below.

Across

3. large mass of ice floating in the ocean
6. ridge of rock at or near the ocean's surface
8. large body of salt water
10. giant waves caused by an earthquake on the ocean floor
11. rise and fall of surface of the ocean
12. the tide when the water reaches its highest point

Down

1. sandy shore washed by tides of oceans
2. mountain rising above the ocean floor
4. body of water surrounded on three sides by land
5. a cliff extending into the ocean
7. another name for *ocean*
9. flow of water in a certain direction

Word List

high tide gulf ocean sea beach current seamount iceberg
sea cliff tsunamis reef tide

Metals

Fill in the spaces with the names of ten metals found on Earth. Choose the names from the list.

3-Letter Word

tin

4-Letter Words

gold
iron
lead
zinc

6-Letter Words

copper
silver
nickel

7-Letter Word

mercury

8-Letter Word

aluminum

SCIENCE ADVENTURES

Making Fossils

Fossils are evidence of life found in rocks. Animal fossils are often preserved shells and bones. Plant fossils include objects such as petrified wood. A fossil need not be the actual remains of a once-living plant or animal. It may be indirect evidence of life, such as preserved tracks or the outline of a plant or animal preserved in rocks formed from mud.

Paleontologists are scientists who collect and study fossils. They use fossils to help them tell the story of what the earth was like millions of years ago.

In this science adventure, you are invited to simulate fossil formation.

What ways can you think of in which fossils might help paleontologists tell about the past?

To make "fossils," you will need different objects, such as leaves, shells, coins, buttons, twigs, seeds, and stones. You will also need plaster of paris, water, and containers such as cupcake cups or disposable pie plates.

First, follow the directions on the plaster of paris box to make a pasty mix. Pour this mix into your containers.

Second, place objects on the plaster as it begins to harden. Remove the objects before the plaster gets too hard. Try to leave a clear impression of the objects on the plaster of paris.

You can make tracks of animals. See if your classmates can tell anything about the animals that made the tracks—size, number of legs, and so forth.

Ask your classmates to tell about an imaginary extinct tribe of people from the fossils you have made.

Writing Science Fiction

In this science adventure, you are invited to participate in the exciting world of science fiction. But remember that today's fiction may be tomorrow's fact.

We have started a little story for you. You can add the products of your own imagination. Have fun!

SURPRISE AT JOURNEY'S END

The journey had been long—three months, to be exact. And it had not been pleasant. There had been problems with the spaceship's cooling system, and then all communication with Earth had been disrupted by magnetic storms for nearly two weeks. But now everything was going smoothly, and Journey's End was in sight on the ship's astrovision screen.

Journey's End was a small planet that scientists on Earth thought might have water, air, and temperature close to that on Earth. But no one knew for sure, because Journey's End was trillions of miles away from Earth. And, for some unknown reason, every time an automatic space probe had been sent out, it stopped sending back information long before it landed on the surface of Journey's End.

There was a bump, and six astronauts moved to the space ports. They looked out and then looked at each other in amazement because

. . . _____

_____

_____

PHYSICAL SCIENCE

Windmills were once used to pump water on many American farms. When electricity became available, farmers replaced their windmills with electric pumps. Today, the rising cost of electric power is causing people to think again about using the power of the wind. New windmills are being built. Some scientists believe that the wind will once more be an important source of power in places where the wind blows steadily and often.

Using the Earth's Heat

Can geothermal energy help solve our energy problems?

The word *geothermal* (jē′ ō thûr′ məl) means "earth heat." There are "hot spots" deep beneath the earth's surface. Sometimes, water seeping into these hot spots is heated and changes to steam. Then, some of the steam and hot water shoot up through cracks in the earth's surface and form *geysers* (gī′ zərz). Other times, the water and steam flow out slowly and form hot springs. These forms of geothermal energy are being used now to produce electricity and to heat buildings in places such as California and Iceland.

But not all of the earth's heat can be seen in the form of geysers or hot springs. Most of it is trapped in pockets of rock under the earth's surface. The trick is to find these pockets and tap the geothermal energy that is there. One method is to drill deep holes in the rock and pump water into the holes. The hot rock heats the water, which rises up through the holes as steam. Then, the steam can be used to drive machines to make electrical energy.

1. The word *geothermal* means
   - a. earth rock.
   - b. earth pocket.
   - c. earth heat.

2. When water seeps into the hot spots under the earth's surface, _____ is formed.
   - a. steam
   - b. electricity
   - c. a pocket

3. According to the story, most of Earth's heat
   - a. shoots up through cracks in the earth's surface.
   - b. is trapped in rock pockets beneath the earth.
   - c. flows slowly to the earth's surface.

4. To tap sources of geothermal energy, which of the following must be done *first*?
   - a. Locate the hot spots under the earth's surface.
   - b. Use steam to make electrical energy.
   - c. Drill holes deep into the earth.

5. What causes the water pumped into the holes to change to steam?
   - a. the heat under the earth's surface
   - b. the heat caused by the drilling
   - c. the electrical energy made by the machines

Trapping the Sun's Rays

Sun power is on the way.

Each day of the year, the sun "comes up" and sends out lots of energy called *solar* (sō′lər) energy. But much of the sun's energy is wasted. Scientists and engineers are trying to find new ways to use solar energy and put it to work in homes and factories.

Solar cells are one way to trap the sun's energy. Solar cells are made of certain chemicals that can change the sun's energy into electricity. Solar cells can be put on the roof of a building. As the sun shines down, its heat energy is changed into electrical energy. The electricity goes through the electrical wires of a building to heat and light it.

Using solar cells to produce electricity can be expensive, but scientists have already found one way to make it cheaper. They are able to collect the sun's rays, make them stronger, and then send these stronger rays, or beams, into the solar cell. That way, each solar cell would produce more electricity more cheaply.

1. Energy from the sun is called _____ energy.
   a. solar
   b. chemical
   c. cell

2. What is in solar cells that changes the sun's rays into electricity?
   a. wires
   b. heat
   c. chemicals

3. In this story, it is the sun's _____ energy that is used to make electricity.
   a. light
   b. chemical
   c. heat

4. What do solar cells do with the sun's energy?
   a. make it stronger
   b. trap and change it
   c. carry it to buildings

5. Why do you think the roof of a building is a good place for solar cells? (Choose the *best* answer.)
   a. It is cheaper to put solar cells on the roof.
   b. A building's electrical wires are on the roof.
   c. The roof usually gets a lot of sunlight.

Rust, a Big Headache

Look all around you. Can you see rust anywhere?

Rust is a problem because it causes things to wear out sooner than they should. Rust forms when iron and oxygen come together. If the object is moist or wet, it will rust more quickly.

Steel is a material made of iron and other things. Because it has iron in it, steel can rust. Therefore, a coating of some sort is put on steel objects to protect them from rust.

One object made of steel is the bumper on a car. Car bumpers are covered with a special metal called *chromium* (krō′ mē əm), which acts like a shield. That is, the chromium coat prevents the car bumper from coming into contact with oxygen. If the chromium is scratched or scraped off, rust will soon appear on the bumper.

Scientists are looking for new ways to control rust. They hope to find ways to protect objects made of steel. If they succeed, then steel objects will last longer.

1. Steel is a material made of
    a. iron and other things.
    b. rust and iron.
    c. oxygen and chromium.

2. What forms when iron and oxygen come together?
    a. steel
    b. chromium
    c. rust

3. Chromium acts as a
    a. car bumper.
    b. special shield.
    c. heavy iron.

4. The *main reason* for using chromium on a car is to
    a. separate oxygen from rust.
    b. keep oxygen away from the steel.
    c. make the car look shiny.

5. Rust is a big headache because it causes
    a. things to wear out more quickly.
    b. cars to keep from starting quickly on wet days.
    c. chromium to scratch more easily.

Trash—A New Energy Source

In some places, trash is being used as fuel.

People throw out trash, or garbage, every day and never think about it. But there is so much trash that it has become a big problem. We are running out of places to put the trash. Now, scientists have discovered a way to make good use of trash.

In certain parts of the country, trash is collected and brought to special *processing plants* (prŏs'ĕs'ĭng plănts'). At the processing plant, machines remove the glass and metal from the trash. This material is sold. Then, the remaining trash is cut up into tiny pieces and put into huge furnaces, where it is burned as fuel.

The burning trash heats water until it becomes steam, and the steam energy drives machines to produce electricity. Finally, the electricity produced at the processing plant is sold to factories or to power companies. Sometimes the steam is also sold.

1. At some *processing plants,* trash is burned as
   - a. steam.
   - b. fuel.
   - c. electricity.

2. What does the processing plant sell besides electricity?
   - a. machines and furnaces
   - b. glass, metal, and steam
   - c. plants and trash

3. Besides trash, what is used in the process described to make electricity?
   - a. glass
   - b. water
   - c. metal

4. Why is trash a good source of fuel?
   - a. There is a large supply of it.
   - b. It contains glass and metal.
   - c. It can be cut up into tiny pieces.

5. Under which of the following headings would you list trash?
   - a. Useless Waste Materials
   - b. A Source of Energy
   - c. An Impossible Problem

The Car of Tomorrow?

The car of tomorrow may run on electric batteries.

In the early 1900s, electric cars were quite popular. They ran quietly and smoothly and did not dirty the air with *pollutants* (pə loot′ nts). But an electric car was slow, and its batteries were very heavy and had to be charged about every 150 kilometers. Soon, the number of electric cars decreased, and gasoline-burning cars took over the roadways.

But the electric car may be making a comeback. It still offers a smooth, quiet ride. And it does not give off the pollutants that gasoline-burning cars do. Scientists and engineers have developed smaller and lighter storage batteries. They are working on a battery that will supply even more electricity to the car's motor, so that the car will run at higher speeds.

There is also the possibility that tomorrow's car may use electric batteries *and* a small gasoline-burning engine. Whatever happens, when all the problems are solved, the gasoline-burning car may go the way of the covered wagon!

1. A *pollutant* is something that
    a. dirties the air.
    b. helps a car ride smoothly.
    c. makes a battery quiet.

2. The batteries in the electric cars from the early 1900s were very
    a. quiet.
    b. heavy.
    c. small.

3. If a battery that supplies more electricity to the car's motor is developed, then
    a. electric cars will travel at greater speeds.
    b. less air-polluting gases will be given off.
    c. the ride will be much smoother.

4. According to the story, scientists are now working on a car that will
    a. run on two kinds of power.
    b. use gasoline as a fuel.
    c. need no motor at all.

5. The last sentence in the story tells us that a gasoline-burning car
    a. will never replace the covered wagon.
    b. may soon be a thing of the past.
    c. will soon be the car of the future.

A Treasure of Bubbles

A big treasure hunt is going on all over the world.

Natural gas is a *fuel* (fyōō′əl). When it burns, it provides energy to heat buildings and make electricity. It also burns without making smoke. Natural gas is sometimes found in the same place as oil. And since we are running out of oil, people thought we were running out of gas, too. But scientists and engineers think that there is enough natural gas to last more than 30,000 years.

Between 5,000 and 10,000 meters under the earth's surface, natural gas is trapped in salt water, rocks, and sand. Engineers are drilling offshore. When they drill deep into the ocean floor, water rushes up and the gas dissolved in the water bubbles out.

Engineers have also found natural gas trapped in coal seams and in sandstone deep in the earth, and in the form of "ice" deep under the Arctic snow.

But there are problems with drilling so deep into the earth. Equipment is very expensive, and often, after drilling for many weeks, the well is "dry." Then engineers start looking and drilling all over again.

1. Something that is burned to provide energy is called a
   _____ .

2. Energy from natural gas is used to heat buildings and make
   a. smoke.
   b. electricity.
   c. oil.

3. According to the story, one advantage to using natural gas is
   that it is
   a. cheaper than oil.
   b. close to the earth's surface.
   c. a clean-burning fuel.

4. When engineers find a dry well, what do they find?
   a. gas trapped in sandstone
   b. gas frozen in ice
   c. no gas at all

5. The story calls the search for natural gas a "treasure hunt"
   because
   a. gas is a valuable fuel hidden beneath the earth's
      surface.
   b. the equipment used to drill for the trapped gas is very
      costly.
   c. natural gas is found with oil, which is very expensive.

Wood, a Resource with Many Lives

Wood is one natural resource that need not be wasted.

Wood is an important *natural resource* (năch′ ər əl rē′ sôrs′), something that is found in nature and is valuable to humans. Wood is used as fuel, as building material, and for making paper and other products. But, for a long time, much of the wood obtained from trees has been wasted. Scientists and engineers are working on new ways to use this natural resource more efficiently.

One way is to change *biomass* (bī′ ō măs), or plant and animal matter, into energy that can be used now. Timber, or wood, waste is a very good source of biomass. In 1979, chemical engineers at a biomass plant in Oregon succeeded in making 1 barrel of oil from 405 kilograms of wood chips. This oil could be burned as fuel for power plants that produce electricity.

In the United States, there are also large forests of fast-growing scrub trees. The wood from these trees cannot be used as building material. But it could be used as biomass to produce energy.

1. Something that is found in nature and is valuable to humans is called a _____.

2. What do we call plant or animal matter that can be used to produce energy?
   a. waste
   b. biomass
   c. electricity

3. List two ways in which wood is used.
   a. _____
   b. _____

4. One way to use wood more efficiently is to
   a. use the wood from scrub trees as building material.
   b. stop making paper products.
   c. use timber waste as a source of energy.

5. Which statement *best* explains the meaning of the story's title, "Wood, a Resource with Many Lives"?
   a. Wood is an important natural resource.
   b. Wood will live on forever and ever.
   c. Wood and wood waste can be used for a variety of purposes.

Travel by Air

Travel by aircraft will soon be quicker, cleaner, and quieter.

Many improvements have been made in the design and construction, or building, of aircraft. Some of the improvements are the result of anti-noise laws. Aircraft must pass noise level inspection before they are allowed to land at certain airports. Scientists and engineers in the field of *aeronautics* (âr′ ə nô′ tĭks) have been working on ways to reduce aircraft noise. Aeronautics is the design and construction of aircraft.

To lessen the noise heard on the ground, aeronautical engineers are designing planes that can land and take off on shorter runways. These planes will make steeper and quicker takeoffs and landings. Some newly designed planes will be able to land and take off almost vertically, like a helicopter. This will mean less noise and air pollution at airports. Also, the need for 300-meter aircraft carriers and large airports will be reduced.

1. The design and construction of aircraft is called _____ .

2. Aircraft must pass _____ inspection before they can land at certain airports.

3. Engineers are designing planes that will have _____ take-offs and landings.
    a. louder
    b. faster
    c. lower

4. The story suggests that if airplanes could land and take off almost vertically, then
    a. helicopters might never be used again.
    b. airport runways would be made longer.
    c. air and noise pollution would decrease at airports.

5. After reading this story, you could say that
    a. aircraft, such as helicopters and planes, make very little noise.
    b. people are always working on ways to improve air travel.
    c. there will always be a need for 300-meter aircraft carriers.

Marie Sklodowska Curie (1867—1934)

Marie Sklodowska was born in Poland in 1867. She went to Paris, France, to study chemistry and physics. While there, she met and later married Pierre Curie, a physicist. The Curies were interested in radioactive materials. Materials that are radioactive give off light rays that are invisible to the human eye. But these rays can go through paper, wood, flesh, and even thin sheets of metal. The Curies wanted to find out what caused radioactive materials to give off invisible rays of light.

They worked for 4 years. In their experiments, they used rocks called pitchblende, which is a kind of uranium ore. The Curies learned that pitchblende is very radioactive. They discovered a special substance in the pitchblende and decided to call it radium. A Nobel Prize was awarded to the Curies for their work.

Later, Marie Curie founded the Radium Institute in Paris. She became the first director of the institute. There, she continued to work to find out more about radium and how it could be used to help human beings. The radiations from radium, for example, can be used to kill harmful bacteria. And radiation is used in the treatment of cancer and some skin diseases.

At the age of 67, Marie Curie died. During her lifetime, she was awarded two Nobel Prizes for her important work.

A Visit to the Brooklyn Children's Museum

It is a place for looking. It is a place for finding. But, most of all, it is a place for doing. The name of the place is the Brooklyn Children's Museum in Brooklyn, New York. It was started in 1899, and it is the oldest children's museum in the world. But you don't have to be a child to enjoy this wonderful place. Adults will love it, too.

The message in this museum is "Hands on." The museum allows visitors to explore and discover on their own. Visitors are encouraged to touch, handle, and play with many objects in the museum.

Visitors can learn about plants, electricity, machines, gravity, and sun and water power. They can discover how a windmill works. With the flip of a switch, a visitor turns on a large fan that blows air across the blades of a real windmill. A water pump, attached to the windmill, draws water from an indoor stream.

Besides machines, visitors can see dolls, fossils, seashells, rocks, and minerals. And there is even a greenhouse where children can grow plants.

PUZZLES TO DO

Solar Energy

Solar energy can be used for heating water, heating your home, cooking, and many other things. Solar energy can be changed into electricity. Find the path from the sun to the lamp on the table.

Electricity

How good are you with electricity? This puzzle contains words that are related to electricity. If you need help, use the words listed below.

Across

1. A _____ turns on or turns off electricity.
5. Large machines that produce electricity are called _____ .
8. A comb rubbed with a wool cloth can produce _____ electricity.
9. An _____ is used to send out and receive radio waves and television waves.
11. Flashlights use _____ .
12. Most metals are good conductors of _____ .

Down

2. Copper _____ is used to build an electric circuit.
3. An _____ prevents the flow of electricity.
4. A tool that measures an electric current is a _____ .
6. Electric current flows through a path called a _____ .
7. A _____ uses electricity to give off light.
10. Electricity is a form of _____ .

Word List

static insulator batteries switch wire energy circuit galvanometer antenna generators lamp electricity

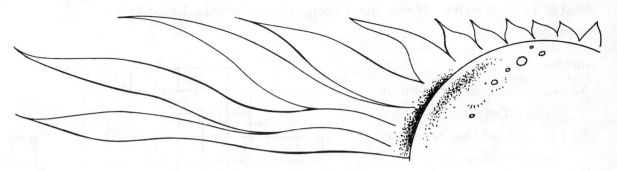

Investigating Solar Energy

Solar energy is energy from the sun. The earth receives huge amounts of solar energy each day from the sun. In fact, scientists have calculated that every 2 weeks, the earth receives more energy from the sun than all of the energy stored in the earth's remaining coal, oil, and natural gas. Unfortunately, however, it is very difficult to put this solar energy to use. Some of the problems involved in utilizing solar energy are:

1. Solar energy is not constant. It varies with cloud cover, it is spread out over the entire surface of the earth, and we get none at night.

2. It is extremely expensive to store solar energy, to use it directly, and to change it into electricity.

In this set of science adventures, you are encouraged to investigate three questions dealing with solar energy:*

1. In collecting solar energy, is bigger better?
2. How much warmer do things get in the sun than in the shade?
3. What color absorbs the sun's heat best?

* Adapted from *Science Activities in Energy*, American Museum of Science and Energy.

In collecting solar energy, is bigger better?

To do this science adventure, you will need two disposable pie plates—a large one and a small one. You will also need some non-water-soluble black paint, a paintbrush, a thermometer, a measuring cup, some clear plastic food wrap, some newspapers, two Styrofoam cups, masking tape, a watch, and water.

1. Paint the pie plates black. After they are dry, put 100 cubic centimeters of water (at room temperature) in each plate. Wrap each plate in plastic wrap, and tape it to hold it on.

2. Put the plates on a stack of newspapers in the sun for 15 minutes.

3. Pour the water from each plate into a Styrofoam cup, and measure the temperature of both cups of water.

What do you observe?
Is bigger better in collecting solar energy?

How much warmer do things get in the sun than in the shade?

To do this science adventure, you will need two Styrofoam cups, two thermometers, a watch, and water.

1. Pour equal amounts of very cold water (from the refrigerator) into two Styrofoam cups.

2. Place a thermometer in each cup.

3. Set one cup in the sun and the other in the shade.

4. Read the temperature on each thermometer each minute for 15 minutes, and record the temperatures on the graph.

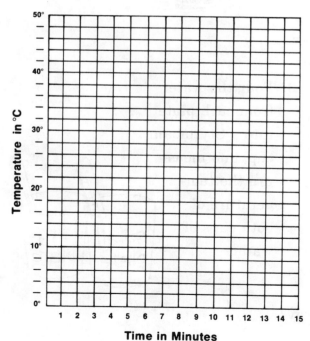

What does your data show?

What color absorbs the sun's heat best?

To participate in this science adventure, you will need four or five pieces of construction paper. They should be the same kind of paper and the same size, but different colors—white, black, green, red, and blue. You will also need uniformly sized ice cubes and a watch.

Place an ice cube on top of each sheet of construction paper in the sun. Which ice cube melts first?

Would you get the same results if you put the ice cubes underneath the paper? Try it out. What do you observe?

WHAT DO YOU THINK?

Would a house with a white roof be cooler than a house with a dark roof?

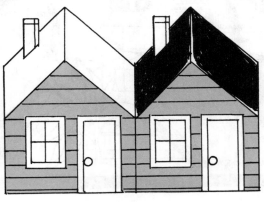

Would a house with a dark roof be more or less expensive to air-condition in the summertime?

CAREERS IN SCIENCE

People are very worried about the world and its natural resources. Until now, we have used those resources without thinking about them. Now, we know we must think about ways to make sure that our children and grandchildren will be able to use those resources, too.

Some career areas that have to do with Earth's resources are:
Ecology
Forestry
Oceanography

Ecologists study how the ecosystem (living things and nature) works and what people must do to keep it working right. Ecologists know that pollution is dangerous. They try to teach people about the environment. They tell factory owners not to dump dangerous chemicals into our rivers and not to pollute the air and the land. Ecologists work with industry and with people to come up with ways to stop pollution.

111

On your way home from school today, look for evidence of pollution.
Make a chart:

Type of Pollution	Cause	What Should Be Done	What I Can Do

Earth's oceans are a major source of food and natural resources.
People who work with and study the ocean are called **oceanographers**.
There are different kinds of oceanographers.

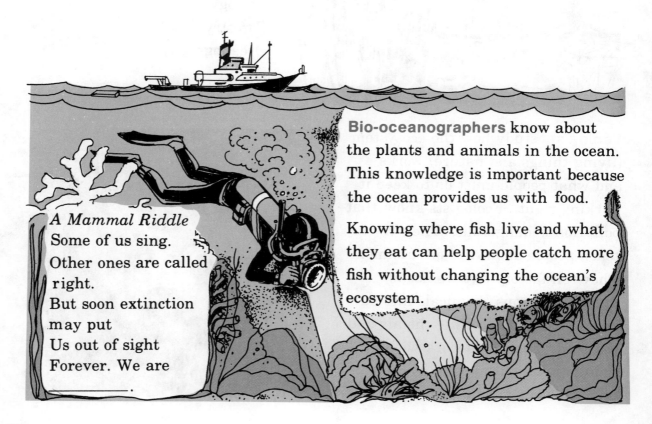

A Mammal Riddle
Some of us sing.
Other ones are called right.
But soon extinction may put
Us out of sight
Forever. We are
_____.

Bio-oceanographers know about the plants and animals in the ocean. This knowledge is important because the ocean provides us with food.

Knowing where fish live and what they eat can help people catch more fish without changing the ocean's ecosystem.

Turn your alphabet on end. Start counting from 1, and solve this code. Then for *more* fun, make one for a friend.

15 — 18 — 21 — 22 _____

25 — 22 — 20 — 26 — 13 _____

18 — 13 _____

7 — 19 — 22 _____

12 — 24 — 22 — 26 — 13 _____

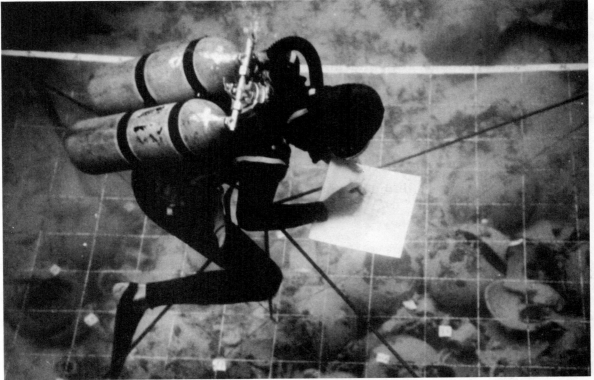

Geo-oceanographers know about the ocean floor and about undersea earthquakes and volcanoes. They know where minerals and other natural resources are.

Some people who work with oceanographers include **divers** and **underwater photographers,** people who operate and take care of ships, and **cartographers** (people who make maps).

Our forests are important natural resources. National and state parks provide places where we can enjoy the outdoors and learn how animals live.

Forests also provide wood, an important resource that gives us many different products.

People who take care of our forests are called foresters.

Foresters know about trees and animals in the forest. They have to know about water, soil, and air, too. All of these are part of the forest ecosystem.

Some of the things foresters do include planting trees; planning roads; and supervising the harvesting, or cutting down and gathering, of trees.

They have to know how to protect our forests from plant and animal diseases, insects that may cause damage, and careless people.

Wood Products

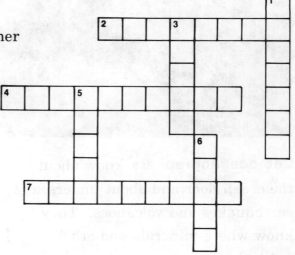

Across

2. One kind is used to draw with, another to cook with.

4. a product used as a paint thinner

7. a product used in making boxes

Down

1. a disinfectant

3. Violinists put it on their bows.

5. what this page is made of

6. Put this on your pancakes.

Word List

alcohol cardboard charcoal paper resin syrup turpentine

Here is a list of tools. Write each tool under the science career in which it would most likely be used. Some tools can be used in more than one career.

irrigation pipe camera
binoculars ruler
poster truck
swim fins saw
Bunsen burner slide projector
audiometer test tube
bulldozer shovel
compass computer
scuba diving axe
   equipment sonar
calipers microscope
barometer ship

Oceanographer	Ecologist	Forester

Here is a familiar object. How many different science careers can you think of that were involved in designing, building, and taking care of this object?

Some things people need to know when they build a house:
kind of land it is on
climate water, sewer
systems, electricity
materials used to
build it

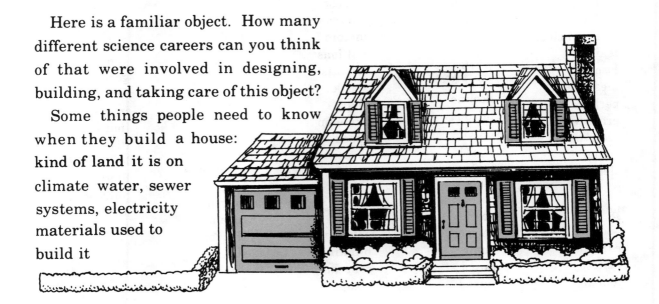

WORDS TO KNOW

The following words are found in the stories throughout this book. The words are listed according to the page on which they appear.

Many of the science books and magazines that you use contain some or all of these words. So it is important that you know the meaning of each word as it is used in science. This will make it easier for you to read and understand science materials.

Use a dictionary or a glossary of science terms to find the meanings and pronunciations of those words that are not familiar to you. You may want to record this information in your own personal "word bank."

LIFE SCIENCE UNIT

p. 14
actions
chemical
daylight
example
fool
heat
include
internal clock
leaves
loses
message
perform
produces
receives
signal
sleepy

p. 16
bodies
extinction
fastest
female

float
grown
heavier
layers
liters
mammal
meters
plankton
pods
produces
surface
travel
whale

p. 18
crops
decline
falcon
hatch
insects
laid
laws
peregrine
pesticide
poisons
quail
raised
ruined

sprayed
survived
terrible

p. 20
attack
bones
cartilage
elastic
especially
human beings
largest
material
meters
millions
scientists
shark
sharp
skeleton
speed
torpedo
tough

p. 22
actually
blinking
conceal
escape

extra
greenish
locate
lowers
organs
purpose
reefs
skin
underneath
upset
usually

p. 24
can't
capybara
centimeters
friendly
gnaw
grown
hind
kilograms
largest
length
rodent
shorter
strange
webbed
weigh

p. 26
aqueous humor
blink
built
contain
cornea
destroys
dirt
drain
duct
eyeball
eyelashes
eyelid
fluid
gently
germs
infection
ingredient
injure
itchy
lens
lifetime
nutrients
overflows
protectors
salty
scientific

known
misunderstood
produce
really
silk
single
species
spinners
spun
strand
stuck
thorax
victims
weave
webs

EARTH-SPACE SCIENCE UNIT

p. 60
action
area
destroy
entire
faster
funnel
narrow
obey
occurs
quickly
rises
shelter
sinks
siren
spin
storm
sucking
tornado
upward

usually
warning

p. 62
amazing
buried
climate
colder
cracks
discovery
formed
forward
freeze
frozen
glacier
intact
known
mammoth
perfectly
period
preserved
remained
scientists
shorter
slowly
thousands
unlucky
weight
wooly

p. 64
backbone
bony
buds
clams
crinoids
crocodiles
evidence
form
fossils
hunters
marine
millions
petal

preserved
proof
recognize
remains
scientists
snails
starfish
states
stems

p. 66
clockwise
counterclockwise
inner
kilometers
known
miniature
moons
numeral
opposite
outer
planet
sequence
solar
system

p. 68
active
body
craters
gas
Io
larger
materials
moons
patches
photographs
photos
planet
powerful
satellite
scientists
spacecraft

thousand
travels
unlike
volcanoes

p. 70
below
brightness
closest
craters
fastest
known
Mercury
moon
objects
planet
revolve
solar
space
sunlit
surface
system
temperature
therefore

p. 72
apart
check
fallen
iron
likely
magnet
metal
meteorite
mixture
peanut
space
stony
truck
weighs

p. 74
bodies
bounce

cloud
colder
difficult
droplets
forms
frost
fuel
gently
heating
layer
level
meters
moist
noticeable
raindrops
result
scary
soil
sunshine
travels
troublesome
tucked
unfortunately
usually

PHYSICAL SCIENCE UNIT

p. 86
cracks
drill
electrical
electricity
energy
flow
form
geothermal
geysers
heat
method
produce
pump

118

rises
seeping
slowly
steam
surface

p. 88
beams
cheaper
cheaply
chemicals
collect
electrical
electricity
energy
engineers
expensive
factories
heat
produce
rays
scientists
solar
solar cells
stronger

p. 90
bumper
chromium
contact
control
forms
iron
longer
material

metal
moist
object
oxygen
prevents
quickly
rust
scientists
scraped
shield
sooner
sort
steel
succeed
therefore

p. 92
certain
collected
electricity
energy
factories
finally
fuel
furnaces
garbage
huge
machines
metal
power
processing
produce
public
remaining
remove

scientists
steam
throw
trash

p. 94
batteries
comeback
decreased
dirty
electric
electricity
engine
engineers
gasoline
higher
kilometers
lighter
pollutants
popular
possibility
quietly
roadways
smaller
smoothly
solved
speeds
storage
supply
whatever

p. 96
bubbles
coal
dissolved
drill

dry
electricity
energy
engineers
equipment
expensive
form
fuel
heat
meters
natural gas
oil
provides
sandstone
scientists
surface
trapped

p. 98
barrel
biomass
cannot
chemical
chips
efficiently
electricity
energy
engineers
fuel
humans
kilograms
material
natural resource
nature
obtained
oil

power
produce
products
scientists
scrub
source
succeeded
timber
valuable

p. 100
aeronautics
aircraft
airports
allowed
antinoise
construction
design
engineers
helicopter
improvements
inspection
laws
lessen
level
meter
newly
pollution
quicker
reduce
result
runways
shorter
steeper
vertically

KEEPING A RECORD OF YOUR PROGRESS

The Progress Charts on these pages are for use with the questions that follow the stories in the Life Science, Earth-Space Science, and Physical Science Units. Keeping a record of your progress will help you to see how well you are doing and where you need to improve. Use the charts in the following way:

After you have checked your answers, look at the first column, headed "Questions Page." Read down the column until you find the row with the page number of the questions you have completed. Put an X through the number of each question in the row that you answered correctly. Add the number of correct answers, and write your total score in the last column in that row.

After you have done the questions for several stories, check to see which questions you answered correctly. Which ones were incorrect? Is there a pattern? For example, you may find that you have answered most of the literal comprehension questions correctly but that you are having difficulty answering the applied comprehension questions. If so, then this is an area in which you need help.

When you have completed all the stories in a unit, write the total number of correct answers at the bottom of each column.

PROGRESS CHART FOR LIFE SCIENCE UNIT

Questions Page	Comprehension Question Numbers				Total Number Correct per Story
	Science Vocabulary	Literal	Interpretive	Applied	
15	1	2	3,4,5		
17	1	2	3,4	5	
19	1	2	3,4,5		
21	1	2	3,4,5		
23	1	2	3,4,5		
25	1	2	3,4,5		
27	1	2,3	4,5		
29	1,2	3	4,5		
31	1	2	3,4	5	
33	1	2	3,4,5		
35	1	2	3	4,5	
37	1	2,3	4,5		
39	1	2,3	4	5	
41	1	2	3,4,5		
43	1	2,3	4	5	
45	1	2	3,4	5	
47	1	2	3,4	5	
49	1	2,3	4,5		
Total Correct by Question Type					

PROGRESS CHART FOR PHYSICAL SCIENCE UNIT

Questions Page	Comprehension Question Numbers				Total Number Correct per Story
	Science Vocabulary	Literal	Interpretive	Applied	
87	1	2,3	4,5		
89	1	2,3	4,5		
91	1	2,3	4,5		
93	1	2	3,4	5	
95	1	2,3	4,5		
97	1	2	3,4,5		
99	1	2,3	4,5		
101	1	2,3	4,5		

Total Correct by Question Type

PROGRESS CHART FOR EARTH-SPACE SCIENCE UNIT

Questions Page	Comprehension Question Numbers				Total Number Correct per Story
	Science Vocabulary	Literal	Interpretive	Applied	
61	1	2,3	4,5		
63	1	2,3	4,5		
65	1	2,3	4	5	
67	1	2,3	4	5	
69	1	2,3	4,5		
71	1	2,3	4	5	
73	1	2	3,4,5		
75	1	2,3	4,5		

Total Correct by Question Type

BIBLIOGRAPHY

Books on Life Science

Bertol, Roland. *Charles Drew*. New York: Crowell, 1970.

Boulton, Carolyn. *Trees*. New York, Watts, 1984.

Casselli, Giovanni. *The Human Body and How it Works*. New York, Putnam, 1987.

Florian, Douglas. *Discovering Trees*. New York, Scribners, 1986.

Halmi, Robert. *Zoos of the World*. New York: Four Winds Press, 1975.

Laycock, George. *Squirrels*. New York: Four Winds Press, 1975.

Leen, Nina. *Snakes*. New York: Holt, 1978.

Leon, Dorothy. *The Secret World of Underground Creatures*. New York: Messner, 1982.

Owen, Jennifer. *Insect Life*. Tulsa, Oklahoma: EDC, 1985.

Patterson, Lillie. *Benjamin Bannecker: Genius of Early America*. illustrated by David Scott Brown. Nashville, Tennessee: Abingdon, 1978.

Pringle, Laurence. *Listen to the Crows*. New York: Crowell, 1976.

Schlein, Miriam. *Giraffe: The Silent Giant*. illustrated by Betty Fraser. New York: Four Winds Press, 1976.

_____. *Project Panda Watch*. New York: Macmillan, 1984.

Selsam, Millicent E. *Tyrannosaurus Rex*. New York: Harper, 1978.

Soucie, Anita Holmes. *Plant Fun: Ten Easy Plants to Grow Indoors*. New York: Four Winds Press, 1974.

Strong, Arline. *Veterinarian, Doctor for Your Pet*. New York: Atheneum, 1977.

Tunis, Edwin. *Chipmunks on the Doorstep*. New York: Crowell, 1977.

Books on Earth-Space Science

Alth, Max and Charlotte. *Disastrous Hurricanes & Tornadoes*. New York: Watts, 1981.

Berger, Melvin. *Oceanography Lab*, Scientists at Work Series. New York: Crowell, 1973.

_____. *The New Air Book*. New York: Crowell, 1974.

Blair, Carvel. *Exploring the Sea: Oceanography Today*. New York: Random House, 1986.

Branley, Franklyn M. *Sunshine Makes the Seasons*. rev. ed. New York: Crowell, 1986.

D'Ignazio, Fred. *The New Astronomy: Probing the Secrets of Space*. New York: Watts, 1982.

Fichter, George S. *Rocks & Minerals*. New York, Random House, 1982.

Gans, Roma. *Rock Collecting*. New York: Crowell, 1984.

Larrick, Nancy. *Rain, Hail, Sleet, and Snow*. New Canaan, Connecticut: Garrard, 1961.

Laycock, George. *Caves*. illustrated by DeVere E. Burt. New York: Four Winds Press, 1976.

Moskin, Marietta. *Sky Dragons & Flaming Swords: The Story of Eclipses, Comets, & Other Strange Happenings in the Sky*. New York: Walker, 1985.

Pollard, Michael. *Air, Water, Weather*. New York, Facts on File, 1987.

Simon, Seymour. *Danger from Below—Earthquakes: Past, Present, and Future*. New York: Four Winds Press, 1979.

_____. *Icebergs & Glaciers*. New York: Morrow, 1987.

Books on Physical Science

Amery, Heather. *The Know How Book of Batteries and Magnets: Safe & Simple Experiments*. Tulsa, Oklahoma: EDC, 1977.

Aylesworth, Thomas G. *Science at the Ballgame*. New York: Walker, 1977.

Berger, Melvin. *The Supernatural: From ESP to UFOs*. New York: Crowell, 1977.

Branley, Franklyn M. *Gravity Is a Mystery*. rev. ed. New York: Crowell, 1986.

_____. *Think Metric*. New York: Crowell, 1974.

Collins, Michael. *Energy for the Twenty-First Century*. New York: Crowell, 1975.

Corbett, Scott. *What About the Wankel Engine?* illustrated by Jerome Kuhl. New York: Four Winds Press, 1974.

Lefkowitz, R. J. *Matter All Around You*. New York: Parents' Magazine Press, 1972.

Lewis, Bruce. *Meet the Computer*. illustrated by Leonard Kessler. New York: Dodd, Mead, 1977.

Schneider, Herman and Nina. *Science Fun with a Flashlight*. New York: McGraw-Hill, 1975.

Sootin, Harry. *Easy Experiments with Water Pollution*. New York: Four Winds Press, 1974.

Veglahn, Nancy. *The Mysterious Rays: Marie Curie's World*. illustrated by Victor Juhasz. New York: Coward, 1977.

Walpole, Brenda. *Movement*, Fun with Science Series. New York: Gloucester Press, 1987.

Weiss, Harvey. *Machines & How They Work*. New York: Crowell, 1983.

_____. *How To Be an Inventor*. New York: Crowell, 1980.

Wilson, Mike and Robin Scagell. *Jet Journal*. New York: Viking, 1978.

METRIC TABLE

This table tells you how to change customary
units of measure to metric units of measure.
The answers you get will not be exact.

LENGTH

Symbol	When You Know	Multiply by	To Find	Symbol
in	inches	2.5	centimeters	cm
ft	feet	30	centimeters	cm
yd	yards	0.9	meters	m
mi	miles	1.6	kilometers	km

AREA

Symbol	When You Know	Multiply by	To Find	Symbol
in^2	square inches	6.5	square centimeters	cm^2
ft^2	square feet	0.09	square meters	m^2
yd^2	square yards	0.8	square meters	m^2
mi^2	square miles	2.6	square kilometers	km^2
	acres	0.4	hectares	ha

MASS (weight)

Symbol	When You Know	Multiply by	To Find	Symbol
oz	ounces	28	grams	g
lb	pounds	0.45	kilograms	kg
	short tons (2000 lb)	0.9	tonnes	t

VOLUME

Symbol	When You Know	Multiply by	To Find	Symbol
tsp	teaspoons	5	milliliters	mL
Tbsp	tablespoons	15	milliliters	mL
fl oz	fluid ounces	30	milliliters	mL
c	cups	0.24	liters	L
pt	pints	0.47	liters	L
qt	quarts	0.95	liters	L
gal	gallons	3.8	liters	L
ft^3	cubic feet	0.03	cubic meters	m^3
yd^3	cubic yards	0.76	cubic meters	m^3

TEMPERATURE (exact)

Symbol	When You Know	Multiply by	To Find	Symbol
°F	Fahrenheit temperature	5/9 (after subtracting 32)	Celsius temperature	°C

METRIC TABLE

This table tells you how to change metric
units of measure to customary units of measure.
The answers you get will not be exact.

LENGTH

Symbol	When You Know	Multiply by	To Find	Symbol
mm	millimeters	0.04	inches	in
cm	centimeters	0.4	inches	in
m	meters	3.3	feet	ft
m	meters	1.1	yards	yd
km	kilometers	0.6	miles	mi

AREA

Symbol	When You Know	Multiply by	To Find	Symbol
cm^2	square centimeters	0.16	square inches	in^2
m^2	square meters	1.2	square yards	yd^2
km^2	square kilometers	0.4	square miles	mi^2
ha	hectares (10,000 m^2)	2.5	acres	

MASS (weight)

Symbol	When You Know	Multiply by	To Find	Symbol
g	grams	0.035	ounces	oz
kg	kilograms	2.2	pounds	lb
t	tonnes (1000 kg)	1.1	short tons	

VOLUME

Symbol	When You Know	Multiply by	To Find	Symbol
mL	milliliters	0.03	fluid ounces	fl oz
L	liters	2.1	pints	pt
L	liters	1.06	quarts	qt
L	liters	0.26	gallons	gal
m^3	cubic meters	35	cubic feet	ft^3
m^3	cubic meters	1.3	cubic yards	yd^3

TEMPERATURE (exact)

Symbol	When You Know	Multiply by	To Find	Symbol
°C	Celsius temperature	9/5 (then add 32)	Fahrenheit temperature	°F